The Christmas
ADVENTure

Linda Sommerville

The Christmas ADVENTure

Published by Faith Alive 365

Copyright © 2011 by Phil and Linda Sommerville

Printed in the United States of America

faithALIVE365
Living God's Best Every Day

Faith Alive 365
5958 Tanus Circle
Rocklin, CA 95677
www.FaithAlive365.com

Table of Contents

Welcome to the Christmas ADVENTure!

What is Advent, you ask?

The term Advent literally means "coming," and it's a time to prepare our hearts for Christ's coming into the world and into our lives. Advent is a traditional season of the church, celebrated by Christians for centuries during the four weeks leading up to Christmas.

This Advent season, God is inviting you to look back with wonder at His arrival on earth, and to look inward and allow your heart to be more deeply connected to Jesus Christ, the Savior and King of Kings.

Throughout the pages of this Advent devotional and activity guide, you'll find activities for families with young children, as well as for individuals and older kids – there's something here for everyone to help you stay focused on Christ throughout the season.

You will also find a weekly guide for having your own home Advent candle lighting ceremony. This simple time of lighting a candle, reading a scripture, and having a meaningful discussion with family or friends can help you stay connected with others and experience the Christ of Christmas together.

This Christmas, in the midst of the inevitable distractions, interruptions, and busyness of the season, you can choose to experience God's presence in deep and meaningful ways. By preparing your head, heart, and hands to encounter Jesus and share Him with others, this can truly be a Christmas to remember.

Oh Come let us adore Him!

Head, Heart & Hands

The Framework for this Advent Guide

The Bible tells us that the reason for Christmas is this: *"For God so loved the world that He gave His one and only Son, that whoever believes in him shall not perish but have eternal life"* (John 3:16).

It all began with the most extravagant gift ever given. God showed up with skin on so that we could know him personally. Immanuel—God with us—is the most remarkable event in history, and we are invited to respond. But how?

Jesus gives us the answer when he says,

> *"'Love the Lord your God with all your heart and with all your soul and with all your mind.' This is the first and greatest commandment. And the second is like it: 'Love your neighbor as yourself"* (Matthew 22:37).

God invites us to respond to His love by worshiping Him with our heads, hearts, and hands. He wants all of us—holding nothing back. He wants us to know Him with our minds, experience Him with our hearts, and serve Him with our hands.

This is the invitation of Christmas, and this is how we can draw near to God during Advent. Each day in this Advent guide, there will be a scripture to read and reflect on (mind), a prayer to pray (heart), and an activity to participate in (hands).

When the Bible speaks about how we worship God in all these ways (head, heart, and hands), it uses the term soul—the total sum of who we are. Let us give Jesus Christ the gift He most desires this Christmas—the gift of our whole selves.

When Does Advent Begin?

Advent traditionally begins four Sundays before Christmas. Since the date varies from year to year, this guide has days of the week rather than dates printed at the top of each page. If Christmas lands on a Sunday, then Advent begins the four Sundays before that.

How <u>Not</u> to Use This Guide

The purpose of this guide is not to add another "to do" to your long list. Feel free to pick and choose which parts of this guide will be most helpful to you—and also feel free to leave some things for next year!

At the beginning of the Advent season, take a few moments to look through this book and think about which items you especially want to include in your celebration. Talk about it with your family, and then schedule them on your calendar.

Likewise, consider which things on your schedule need to be taken off the calendar this month to make room in your life to celebrate a Christ-centered Christmas. You'll also want to be sure and leave some margin in your schedule for the unexpected things that are sure to pop up.

It's important not to try and do it all—or to try and do everything perfectly. The most important thing is to stay open to the mystery and wonder of the season and watch for the ways God will show up in your life.

◎ Weekly Themes ◎

Throughout Advent, this guide will help you focus on different aspects of the season and prepare your heart for Christ's coming.

Week	Theme
Advent Week 1	Preparing the Way of the Lord
Advent Week 2	Welcoming the Lord
Advent Week 3	Paying Attention to the Lord
Advent Week 4	Worshiping the Lord

Sundays In Advent

Each Sunday, in place of activities for your "HANDS", you'll find questions to discuss over a Sunday meal. Talk about them with your family, spouse, roommate, or other friends. These questions will help you evaluate choices and follow through on your desire to keep Christ at the center of your celebration.

Also, on Sundays you will find a simple Advent candle lighting ceremony that can be used with your home Advent wreath (see directions for making a wreath on the next page). This ceremony can help mark the passing weeks, and remind you of the significance of the season.

(Note: there are three pages in this guide for Sundays, and two pages for all other days.)

Making An Advent Wreath

Making an Advent wreath can be a fun project for families or individuals—though if you prefer, you can also purchase one from a Christian bookstore or online. Children especially love tradition and ceremony, and using an Advent wreath to countdown the weeks to Christmas can be a meaningful way to prepare your hearts for His coming.

You may want to place the wreath on your dining table for easy use during mealtimes, and to serve as a reminder of your commitment to celebrate a Christ-centered Christmas.

Materials:

- Foam wreath form or circle, or 12" cardboard circle
- Four candles (8" or taller). If using cardboard, place the candles in small holders.
- Larger white candle (the "Christ" candle) for center
- Aluminum foil
- Real or artificial greenery, Christmas flowers, and so on
- Hot-glue gun

Directions for Foam Wreath:

1. Lay the wreath flat on a table and push the candles into the top in an evenly spaced order.
2. Remove the candles and line the candle holes with aluminum foil.
3. Push short pieces of greenery into the foam wreath. Cover wreath completely, keeping pieces short in order to prevent them from catching fire from lighted candles. Leave room for Christ Candle in the center.
4. Put hot glue on the ends of the candles and press them back into their holes.
5. Set white Christ candle in the center of ring. Use a holder, saucer, or a pad of foil if you are using a wreath form instead of a solid circle of foam.

Directions for Cardboard Wreath:

1. Mark the four places where your candle holders will stand.
2. Cover your cardboard with artificial greenery or flowers, gluing them in place on the cardboard and leaving space for the candle holders. Keep pieces short to prevent them from catching fire from lighted candles.
3. Set the candle holders in place. For added stability, you may want to tape or glue the holders to the cardboard.
4. Set the Christ candle in the center of the ring in a holder, saucer, or on a pad of foil.

NOTE: Always supervise children carefully during candle lighting and never leave them alone with lit candles.

~ **First Week of Advent** ~

Preparing
the Way of the Lord

First Sunday of Advent

Preparing
the Way of the Lord

Questions to Discuss over the Sunday Meal

Gather with family or friends over a meal and talk together about how you can prepare the way of the Lord in your lives and celebrate a Christ-centered season. For families with younger children, select which questions will be most appropriate.

1. What did you like best about some of your recent Christmas celebrations? What did you like least?

2. What are 2-3 Christmas events or activities you wouldn't want to miss? (Take time now to put them on your schedule.) How can Christ be at the center of those?

3. If you could eliminate an activity or two from your schedule this season, what would it be and why?

4. How can you create margin for the unexpected interruptions that will come?

5. Think for a few moments about what you can do when you face distractions and disappointments this season. What will you say to yourself and others? To God? How will you stay Christ-focused when things don't go as planned?

6. For Mary, saying "yes" to God meant surrendering whatever expectations she may have had for her future and opening herself up to God's plans. What expectations for this season do you need to surrender to God? While making plans for celebrating this season, how can you stay open to God's plans? How can you prepare the way of the Lord in your life this season by saying "yes" to God?

Preparing
the Way of the Lord

Advent Candle Lighting
for families with young children (read the following out loud)

Parent: Today we light the first candle in our Advent wreath.

Children: Christmas is coming!

Parent: God is inviting us to slow down and prepare our hearts to celebrate Jesus' birth.

Children: Christmas is coming!

Parent: When the angel told Mary she was going to have a baby, she opened her heart to God. She said "yes" to God and welcomed His plans for her life.

Children: Christmas is coming!

Parent: Even though Mary knew the days ahead might be hard, she prepared the way of the Lord. She traveled to visit her cousin Elizabeth and they talked together about God and prepared for Jesus' birth.

Children: Christmas is coming!

Parent: As we light this candle in our Advent wreath, we promise to slow down, too. We promise to prepare the way of the Lord by opening our hearts to Him and taking time to remember what's most important this Christmas.

(Light the first candle)

All together: Christmas is coming!

Preparing

the Way of the Lord

Advent Candle Lighting

for individuals, couples, or families with older children

Candlelighting: As we light the first candle, we begin our celebration of Advent. In this moment, we slow down our hearts and minds to focus on God and prepare the way of the Lord in our lives this season.

(Light first candle)

New Testament Scripture: Read Luke 1:26-45

Reflection: The news Mary received from the angel must have been shocking and confusing—but her heart was open to God. After the angel reminded her that "nothing is impossible with God," Mary responded by saying, "May it be to me as you have said." This was her way of saying "yes" to God. Mary then prepared herself for God's plan by seeking out her cousin Elizabeth. Together they talked about what God was doing and took time to reflect on the Christmas miracle coming into the world.

Prayer: Father, please help us make room in our hearts for Your coming this season. Help us to prepare for Your coming by slowing down and focusing on You. And like Mary, help us to say "yes" to Your plans in our lives. No matter what this season holds, let us hold on to You and keep You at the center of our celebrations. Amen.

Old Testament Scripture: Isaiah 7:14

Sing: Sing or listen to a favorite Christmas carol.

Slowing Down

Today's Scriptures:

"Be still and know that I am God." (Psalm 46:10)

"And Mary said: 'My soul glorifies the Lord and my spirit rejoices in God my Savior.'" (Luke 1:46-47)

Head
Thought to Ponder:

Mary took time to slow down and prepare her heart for the coming of Christ. After she learned that she was pregnant, she traveled to visit her cousin Elizabeth—who was pregnant with John the Baptist. The two women spent time together talking about God's plans and what was to come. Mary found encouragement and support from Elizabeth as she prepared for the birth of Jesus. Mary also focused her heart on God by praising Him and remembering who He is.

As you begin this Advent season, consider who might be an "Elizabeth" in your life. Who can give you support and encouragement to focus on God and celebrate a Christ-centered Christmas? Make plans to connect with that person in the coming days and weeks, encouraging each other to follow through on your plans for keeping your focus on Jesus. Also consider how can you slow down today and focus more on God. Take time to remember who God is and praise Him, just as Mary did.

Heart
Invitation to Pray:

Lord, we praise You and thank You for loving us so much that You sent Your Son to earth. Please help us slow down this week and focus on You. Help us to remember that we don't have to go through the day on our own—You are Immanuel, God with us, and we are never alone. Help us to be still and know that You are God and You are good. Amen.

Hands

Pick one or two activities that can help you and your family keep a Christ-centered focus.

Time Out   Create a "Time Out" room (not for discipline but for slowing down). Whenever someone from the family goes into that area, they are not to be disturbed except for emergencies. We all need some time to be alone with God. We need a break from the busy and loud activities of the season to simply be with Jesus.

Christmas Kiss Countdown Calendar   Take a long piece of plastic wrap, colored ribbon, and enough candy kisses for each day from now till Christmas. Lay out a long piece of plastic wrap on a table, then place the kisses in a single line lengthwise on the plastic. Roll plastic tightly around the kisses in a long roll, twisting the plastic between each piece. To hold candy in place, tie a ribbon between each piece. Then each day have your children untie one kiss to countdown the days in sweet style. Make it a game to "slow" down and instead of eating the chocolate quickly, let it slowly dissolve on your tongue.

A Chair for Jesus   At dinner time, put an extra chair at the table for Jesus. Use this visual cue to help you slow down and remember that He is there with you.

Hide God's Word   Consider memorizing God's word this season and hiding it in your heart. Before each meal, remain standing behind your chairs and recite a verse of the Luke 2 Christmas story (or another selected passage). Add a new verse every few days and recite the entire passage up to that point. By Christmastime, you'll be able to tell the story from memory.

Get Puzzled   Set up a puzzle on a table for everyone to work on. Invite visitors who come to your home throughout the season to help with it. Use this time to slow down and enjoy each other's company.

Down-sizing Your Life

Today's Scriptures:

"Love the Lord your God with all your heart and with all your soul and with all your strength. These commandments that I give you today are to be upon your hearts. Impress them on your children. Talk about them when you sit at home and when you walk along the road, when you lie down and when you get up." (Deuteronomy 6:4-7)

Head
Thought to Ponder:

God longs to give us a Christmas filled with more of His peace, joy, and love. But as today's scripture reminds us, we must intentionally place God at the center of our lives this season so that we can receive all the good gifts He has to give us. This may mean down-sizing some of our expectations and activities to make more room for Him in our lives.

Consider the following questions: Who are you trying to please or satisfy with your Christmas plans this year? Does any part of your Christmas celebration plans cause you apprehension? How can you eliminate or change your plans to relieve your fears, reduce your stress, and place Christ at the center of your season?

Heart
Invitation to Pray:

Father, please forgive me for the ways that I expect the wrong things from the Christmas season. Help me to reduce the clutter in my life so that there is room for more of You in my life this season. May Your life be born in me today. Amen.

Song to Sing:
Joy to the world! The Lord is Come;
let earth receive her King;
let every heart prepare him room,
And heaven and nature sing *(repeat 2X).*

 ## Hands

Pick one or two activities that can help you and your family keep a Christ-centered focus.

New Year's Letters Instead of sending Christmas cards this year, consider down-sizing your "To Do" list by sending New Year's letters instead. Not only will this downsize your activities, it will also allow you to respond to Christmas cards and gifts received during the season.

Young kids Toy Swap Many kids have more toys in their closet than they ever play with. To encourage the spirit of giving in your children, and to help them get into the down-sizing spirit, have them go through their toys and find several in good shape that they no longer play with. Ask your children to select several toys they can give away to make room for the new toys they will receive at Christmas. Then find a local shelter collecting gifts for needy families—and if possible, take your kids with you to deliver their donations. This will allow your kids the chance to experience the joy of giving firsthand.

The Simplify Game Play the "Simplify Game" by asking yourself and your family these questions: How can we reduce clutter, busyness, and distraction a little bit each day this week? What will we give up to make room for the Christ-child in our celebrations? As you think of specific ideas, write them on slips of paper and crumple them up—then symbolically surrender them to God by throwing them into a trash can or fireplace. Cheer and give points for each "simplify" paper that makes it in.

YouTube—Prepare Ye The Way Remember the 1970's production of GodSpell? Even though this isn't a "Christmas" musical, you can go to YouTube.com and watch a clip of the song "Prepare Ye The Way" —a song sung by John the Baptist, calling people to prepare their hearts for the coming of Christ. This melody will stay with you throughout the day and help you remember to keep your heart open to Him.

Minimizing Distractions

Today's Scriptures:

"Delight yourself in the Lord; and He will give you the desires of your heart. Commit your way to the Lord, trust in Him, and He will do it. Rest in the Lord and wait patiently for Him." (Psalm 37:4-5, 7, NASB)

"In those days John the Baptist came, preaching in the Desert of Judea and saying 'Repent, for the kingdom of heaven is near.' This is he who was spoken of through the prophet Isaiah; 'A voice of one calling in the desert, 'Prepare the way for the Lord, make straight paths for him.''" (Matthew 3:1-3)

Head
Thought to Ponder:

Distractions are inevitable. It's not a matter of *if* they will happen—it's a matter of how we will respond to them *when* they happen. What are some kinds of distractions that were a challenge for you last Christmas season? What kinds of distractions do you anticipate might be a challenge for you this year?

When we prepare the way for the Lord in our lives, we'll be more prepared to respond to distractions in God-honoring ways. One of the ways we prepare the way of the Lord in our lives is by making straight paths for Him, which involves removing barriers that might block God's work in our lives. What things in your life might be barriers to the Lord coming fully into your life today? How can you remove those barriers and prepare the way of the Lord?

Heart
Invitation to Pray:

.Father, help me to recognize the barriers in my life today that might block your work in my life. Help me to remove those barriers and minimize anything that might distract me from You. Amen.

Hands

Pick one or two activities that can help you and your family keep a Christ-centered focus.

Reducing the TV Trap   There are lots of fun Christmas shows to watch this season, but too much TV can add to our stress and increase our appetites for every new toy and gadget being advertised. Be selective about which programs to watch, and avoid watching any "live TV" during this season. Record your shows so that you can fast forward over the commercials. (Unless you play the "Commercial Game" below.)

The Commercial Game   Young kids can have a hard time distinguishing between cartoons and commercials, especially when the ads are selling spin-off characters and toys from your kid's TV shows. Commercials create a sense of dissatisfaction in kids, making them want more. Help your kids by watching some TV with them, and every time a commercial comes on have your kids call out, "Commercial!" — to help them get in the habit of identifying ads. Then help your kids learn to understand the messages in these ads by asking questions like: What is this commercial trying to tell us is most important? What is this commercial telling us about how to be happy? About what we need in our lives? Are these messages all true?

Make a "JOY Jar"   Each day, think about what you've seen God do that day. What are you thankful for? What brought you joy today? Make a "Joy Jar", and have family members write their joys on slips of paper to be placed in the joy jar each day leading up to Christmas. On Christmas Day, open the jar and share the joy with the whole family.

House Blessing   Pray a blessing over your home as a way to prepare your heart and home to be Christ-centered throughout the season. Invite your family and/or a few friends to go though each room of your home praying for the activities that will take place in each room, and for the people who will gather there. (For example, pray God's blessing on your front door that those who enter your home will feel welcomed and will sense God's presence and love as they enter.)

Reliquishing Control

Today's Scriptures:

"And so John came, baptizing in the desert region and preaching a baptism of repentance for the forgiveness of sins." (Mark 1:4)

"When the people heard this, they were cut to the heart and said to Peter and the other apostles, 'Brothers, what shall we do?' Peter replied, 'Repent and be baptized, every one of you, in the name of Jesus Christ for the forgiveness of sins.'" (Acts 2:37-38)

Head
Thought to Ponder:

God's plans are from of old. Even before Adam and Eve committed the first sin, God was already planning the way for Jesus Christ to enter history and bring us back into relationship with Him. But as John the Baptist reminds us in today's scripture, in order to participate in God's good plans we need to prepare the way of the Lord in our lives by receiving His forgiveness.

Today, consider God's plans for your life. Remember that He knew you before you were born. He's inviting you to relinquish control of your life and accept His love and forgiveness. Where might God want you to trust Him more today by letting go of control? What are you holding onto today that you need to let go of? As you relinquish these things, receive Christ's forgiveness and peace.

Heart
Invitation to Pray:

Father, thank You that from the beginning of time You were already making a way for me to have a relationship with You. Thank You that through Christ's forgiveness, I can draw close to You today. Help me to extend that forgiveness to others in my life. I relinquish my desire for control, and I humbly accept your good plans in my life this season. Amen.

Hands

Pick one or two activities that can help you and your family keep a Christ-centered focus.

Reminder Nail   Christ was born so that one day He could die for our sins. In today's verse, John the Baptist reminds us that when we repent and seek Christ's forgiveness, we can have new life. To keep this important message central in your celebration, go to a hardware store and purchase a large nail or spike, tie a ribbon around it and hang it on a center branch of your Christmas tree as a reminder of Christ's death on the cross.

Hand Wreath   Trace and cut out green paper hands for each family member. Color a paper plate green. Each day this season when someone in the family does something kind or loving, write their action on one of their cut-out hands and glue it onto the wreath. Continue doing this each day until the wreath is all covered. Let these hands represent opening your hands to God's plans and sharing His love with others. By Christmas you'll see the many ways your family has shared God's love and stayed focused on Him.

Offer a Christmas Pardon   At Christmas, many state governors offer pardons to certain prisoners as a special act of clemency. Maybe you could do the same. To celebrate the forgiveness Christ offers us, you can honor Christ by pardoning someone you have locked out of your life. Who in your life needs your forgiveness? Write on a piece of paper that person's offense and what you feel is owed to you. Then write out, "I (your name) grant clemency to (his/her name) on (date)" Begin to live in accordance with your declaration and enjoy the new freedom forgiveness can bring.

Silent Retreat   Consider taking a personal silent retreat for one or two days this season. This can be a great way to slow down and center yourself during a busy time of year. There are numerous retreat centers across the country—check online for listings of retreat centers near you.

Welcoming the Lord

Today's Scriptures:

"That is why waiting does not diminish us, any more than waiting diminishes a pregnant mother. We are enlarged in the waiting. We, of course, don't see what is enlarging us. But the longer we wait, the larger we become, and the more joyful our expectancy." (Romans 8:23-24, Message)

"For in this hope we were saved. But hope that is seen is no hope at all. Who hopes for what he already has? But if we hope for what we do not yet have, we wait for it patiently." (Romans 8:24, NIV)

Head
Thought to Ponder:

Hoping and waiting—these two ideas are inseparable. But although we want to be hopeful, we don't like to wait. We live in the age of "instant everything," and waiting is seen as an unbearable inconvenience, something to be avoided at all cost. At this time of year, children especially do not like waiting. Christmas is coming, with the promise of treats and toys, and each day of waiting seems like an eternity.

Adults aren't much better at waiting than children, and that can tempt us to lose hope. But our capacity for love and joy increases as we wait. When our hope is fixed firmly in the truth of God's word and the presence of Christ in our lives, we're able to stay hopeful even in the midst of difficult circumstances. What circumstances are you facing today that might tempt you to give up hope or lose patience with waiting on God?

Heart
Invitation to Pray:

Thank you, Lord, that my hope is not in things or in circumstances. My hope is in You. Help me to wait on You today and trust in Your plans. Amen.

Song To Sing:
O little town of Bethelehem, how still we see thee lie!
Above thy deep and dreamless sleep the silent stars go by
Yet in thy darkness shineth the everlasting Light;
The hopes and fears of all the years are met in thee tonight.

 ## Hands

Pick one or two activities that can help you and your family keep a Christ-centered focus.

Pregnant with God   It's amazing to think about Mary being pregnant with God. How might God want to be born in your life today? As you go through your day, pay attention to any infants you might see. If your kids are with you, make a game out of noticing as many babies as you can—or consider signing up to help in your church nursery this week. Reflect on how God came to us in the form of a helpless infant. Notice a child's tiny hands, toes, and eyelashes. Let it be a reminder that God loves you so much that He took on flesh and blood to be born into our world. Pray for that child and their parents, and thank God for the hope we have because He came to earth as Immanuel—God with us.

Unpack the Nativity   To help us hear the Christmas story as if for the first time, it's great to share it with little ones. Unpack your nativity scene and as you unpack it talk about the story with your kids. If you don't have kids, invite some over to help you arrange your nativity set. If you don't have a nativity set, this might be the year to purchase one. Talk about each character in the story.   What were they thinking and feeling? What did the scene smell and sound like? What would catch your attention? Hear the story yourself as if you were a child, and remember that this is God's fresh hope for the world.

Handel's Messiah   Many communities have performances of Handel's Messiah at this time of year. This inspirational music can help focus your heart on God's goodness as you wait and hope in Him this season. Check local listings to attend a performance in your area—or look for an open "Messiah sing-along" in your community and consider participating.

Puzzling Circumstances   When doing a puzzle as a family, talk about how God sometimes sends circumstances into our lives that puzzle us. But like Mary and Joseph, we can trust that God has a plan, and He will help us put all the pieces together.

Breathing in the Moments

Today's Scriptures:

"Even youths grow tired and weary, and young men stumble and fall; but those who hope in the Lord will renew their strength. They will soar on wings like eagles; they will run and not grow weary, they will walk and not be faint." (Isaiah 40: 30-31)

"Find rest, O my soul, in God alone; My hope comes from him.
He alone is my rock and my salvation; He is my fortress, I will not be shaken." (Psalm 62:5-6)

"Come to me, all you who are weary and burdened, and I will give you rest. Take my yoke upon you and learn from me, for I am gentle and humble in heart, and you will find rest for your souls. For my yoke is easy and my burden is light." (Matthew 11:28-30)

Head
Thought to Ponder:

Even when we're trying to live with balance, we still get weary and tired—especially during this busy and stressful time of year. Celebrating a Christ-centered Christmas means recognizing our limits and leaning on our unlimited God. Today He promises to give strength to the weary. Where are you weary right now, needing His strength? Where are you exceeding your limits today? Ask God to show you how to live with more balance. Trust Him with your "to do's," lean on Him and let Him restore you.

Heart
Invitation to Pray:

Lord Jesus, today I need your strength. Help me to lean on You, to hope in You, to rest in You, to learn from you, and to be filled up with more of You today. Amen.

Hands

Pick one or two activities that can help you and your family keep a Christ-centered focus.

"Breathing" Prayers   To help you soak in God's presence, try this simple prayer exercise. Relax your body and as you breathe out, imagine that you are breathing out all your stress, fears, and worry—offer it up to God. As you breathe in, open yourself up to breathe in more of God—let Him fill you up with more of His peace, love, and presence.

The Gift of "Wasted Time"   While waiting in line at the grocery store (when you choose the "wrong" line), or while waiting for the stoplight to change, or while waiting for your bagel to defrost in the microwave— take a deep breath. Instead of tapping your foot and anxiously thinking about how this is inconveniencing you, slow down. Pray for a family member. Turn on some music and sing a praise song. Use this gift of "wasted" time to focus on God and enjoy Him.

Have An Unplugged Night   Turn off every TV screen, computer, and phone in your home. Play games. Sing songs. Tell someone you love them. Bake. Make a Christmas tree ornament. Call someone and really listen. Tell someone you love them. Pop popcorn. Read a story to the kids. Tell someone you love them. Go for a walk. Make hot chocolate. Hold someone's hand. Tell someone you love them.

In The Moment   This week see how much you can live "in the moment" each day. Look for ways that God is working in each moment, speaking, providing, and encouraging you. When you're in conversations with others, pay attention to what's going on in your heart and mind. How can you be more "present" with them?   Notice when your body is giving you signs of fatigue—then take a nap or go for a walk.

~ Second Week of Advent ~

Welcoming
the Lord

Second Sunday of Advent

Welcoming the Lord

Questions to Discuss over the Sunday Meal

Gather with family or friends over a meal and talk together about how you can welcome the Lord as you celebrate a Christ-centered season. For families with younger children, select which questions will be most appropriate.

1. If Jesus were coming to your house, what special touch might you add to make certain He would feel welcome?

2. If Jesus sat down at the table with you, what might you change in your conversation?

3. In a very real sense, Jesus was a stranger here on earth. What kinds of people did God pick to welcome Him? (Name as many as you can from the Christmas story.) What did these choices say about the kind of ruler He would become?

4. If a young couple like Mary and Joseph came to your door looking for shelter, would you welcome them? Why or why not?

5. What are some of the reasons we hesitate to invite others to join us in our Christmas activities? How can we overcome these reasons?

6 What good things do friends offer to us when we open our hearts and homes? What good things might a stranger bring to our Christmas celebration?

7. Who are some people that Jesus might want you to include in your Christmas activities this year?

Welcoming the Lord

Advent Candle Lighting

for families with young children (read the following out loud)

Parent: *(Parent lights the first candle or assists child to light it.)* Before we light the second candle, let's see if we can remember what the first candle reminded us to do. *(Let kids try to answer.)* The first candle reminded us to prepare the way of the Lord. Today we will light the second candle to remind us to welcome the Lord.

Children: Welcome, Lord Jesus!

Parent: Jesus was born in a stable because there was no room in the inn. They did not welcome Mary and Joseph that night, so Jesus was born where the donkeys and sheep lived.

Children: Welcome, Lord Jesus!

Parent: But that night, the angels came to the shepherds and told them the good news that Jesus was born—and the shepherds rushed off to Bethlehem to welcome Jesus to the world.

Children: Welcome, Lord Jesus!

Parent: When Jesus grew up, He taught us to welcome Him into our lives by welcoming others. Jesus said that when we show God's love to "the least of these," we are showing love to Jesus Himself.

Children: Welcome, Lord Jesus!

Parent: As we light the second candle in our Advent wreath, we open our hearts to welcome Jesus, and we open our hearts to welcome others by sharing His love.

(Light the second candle)

All together: Welcome, Lord Jesus!

Welcoming the Lord

Advent Candle Lighting

for individuals, couples, or families with older children

Candlelighting: *(After lighting the first candle)* Today, as we light the second candle in our Advent wreath, let us remember that Jesus was born because of God's love for the *entire* world. He came for everyone—from the rich and powerful to the poor and needy. And one of the best ways for us to welcome Jesus into our celebrations this season is to welcome others. Let's remember that God loves parties, and He's inviting the whole world to the birthday celebration of His Son. May the lighting of this candle open our hearts up to extend that same kind of welcome to others and shine the light of His love into a dark world.

(Light second candle)

New Testament Scripture: Read Luke 2:1-20

Reflection: Jesus was the King of kings, yet He was not born in a palace. There was not even room for Him at the inn, so He was born in a smelly stable. And as God became human, the party invitations went out to an unlikely group of guests—the shepherds. After the angels announced the birth of Christ and welcomed the shepherds to the celebration, these blue collar workers were the first ones to welcome Jesus into the world. God gives us opportunities to welcome Him into the world, too, as we welcome others. When we do this, it's amazing how often our guests will bring to us unexpected gifts of hope and joy as well.

Prayer: Lord Jesus, You tell us that when we show love to "the least of these," we show love to You. May we welcome You into our lives this season by welcoming others and shining Your light into our world Amen.

Old Testament Scripture: Isaiah 58:6-11

Sing: Sing or listen to a favorite Christmas carol.

Social Networking In Christ

Today's Scriptures:

"The Word became flesh and blood, and moved into the neighborhood." *(John 1:14, Message)*

"Therefore, as God's chosen people, holy and dearly loved, clothe yourselves with compassion, kindness, humility, gentleness, and patience… And whatever you do, whether in word or deed, do it all in the name of the Lord Jesus, giving thanks to God the Father through Him." *(Colossians 3:12, 17)*

Head
Thought to Ponder:

Jesus was the ultimate social networker! He humbled Himself by taking on flesh and blood so that He could "move into the neighborhood." Our God is not a distant God. He is up close and personal, entering our world and our neighborhoods so that we can know Him personally. He took the first step to build a relationship with us, and He calls us to do the same toward others.

Who can you take the fist step with today? Who do you know that may need an encouraging word from you? Are there family or friends living at a distance—because of their jobs or other circumstances—who might be lonely and in need of your time and attention? Is there someone in your neighborhood who might not have family in the area and could use a welcoming invitation to join in on some of your holiday celebrations? Pray for God to bring to your attention those people He wants you to reach.

Heart
Invitation to Pray:

Lord Jesus, today I need your strength. Help me to lean on You, to hope in You, to rest in You, to learn from you, and to be filled up with more of You today. Amen.

Hands

Pick one or two activities that can help you and your family keep a Christ-centered focus.

Family Facebook Page Create a family Facebook page to keep your extended family in contact during the holidays. You can create a special protected page that only your family can see—a place where you can share photos of your seasonal activities, send loving posts to others, and help family members who live at a distance stay connected with you.

SKYPE Your Advent Celebration Another great way to stay connected with family and friends is to use SKYPE (a free web-based video chat service). Consider using SKYPE to share your Advent candle lighting ceremony with distant family.

Decorating party Help a shut-in who can't physically decorate their own home this year. Bring them a Christmas tree, and if they don't have decorations of their own, consider sharing some of yours or perhaps making some decorations. Make plans to come back after Christmas to take down all the decorations and store them away for next year.

Voicemail Greetings Extend a joyful welcome to those who call this season by putting a Christmas greeting on your voicemail. (Consider letting the kids get in on the creative greeting.)

Cookie Swap Invite the neighbors over for a cookie swap. Ask each family to bring a dozen cookies and a copy of the recipe for each family who will be there. Serve hot chocolate, sing Christmas carols, exchange cookies, and let the kids decorate homemade or store-bought sugar cookies. Read the Christmas story. Keep it simple and informal—relax, visit, share, and ENJOY.

Presence Presents As you encounter people today, pass along the gift that keeps on giving, the gift you can even give to the person who "has everything." Pass along the gift of Jesus' presence by silently praying "Stealth prayers" of blessings on others.

Surprising Others

Today's Scriptures:
"That night there were shepherds staying in the fields nearby, guarding their flocks of sheep. Suddenly, an angel of the Lord appeared among them, and the radiance of the Lord's glory surrounded them. They were terrified." (Luke 2:8-9)

Head
Thought to Ponder:

Christmas is a story of good surprises. The shepherds were suddenly surprised by angels. The wise men were surprised by a star. Mary was surprised by a stranger at the door. Joseph was surprised (shocked even) at the news of Mary's pregnancy, and even more shocked at the reason. Mary and Joseph were surprised by unexpected guests. Jesus was full of surprises Himself. His forgiveness is a surprise, as was His crucifixion and then His resurrection.

Our God is a God of surprises. Maybe we have lost some of the wonder and joy of the season because we have lost the sense of surprise. So— do something about it. Surprise people this season through actions and words that bring smiles to their faces. Who can you surprise today?

Heart
Invitation to Pray:

Lord Jesus, thank You for the amazing surprises You bring every day. Help me to keep my eyes and ears open today to recognize the surprises You will bring into my life. And help me to pass Your joy along to others by showing Your love in surprising ways. Amen.

Hands

Pick one or two activities that can help you and your family keep a Christ-centered focus.

Surprising Childcare   Single-parenting can be very stressful during the holidays. Consider offering a full day of free childcare to a single parent you know, allowing them time to do some Christmas shopping or simply to rest.

Popcorn Treasure Balls   Surprise your family by making popcorn balls for a special snack. Inside each ball, hide a treasure—a small toy or treat (ring pops make great items to hide). Share with your kids how this is a reminder that Jesus tells us to "seek and you will find" Him. When we seek God, He is always close, ready to meet our needs and surprise us with His presence and provision.

Pajama Run   After your kids are tucked into bed, surprise them by getting them back up for a surprise "Pajama Run." Keep everyone in their PJ's, and go for a drive to look at Christmas lights. Take along a thermos of hot cocoa. Keep an eye out for how many nativity scenes you can spot. Talk about how God is a God of surprises. What are some of the ways God surprised people in the Christmas story? How might He surprise us?

A Surprise Admiration Gift   This season, if someone admires something of yours, consider giving that item to them as a gift. This thoughtful gift will be a way to down-size and simplify your life while blessing someone else.

Your Own Story   Gather your kids for a story time and begin telling them a story of a family that God loves very much. As you tell your own family's history, leave out specific names (just talk about "the little girl" or "the mommy," etc). Share stories of ways God has worked in your family's life. For example, maybe one Christmas your son had a high fever and you weren't sure what was wrong. Share the worry and dangers involved. Tell about people who prayed and how God answered prayers. Your kids will enjoy the stories—especially as they begin to realize that the family you're talking about is their own! When they do, let them help you tell the stories.

Sharing the Joy

Today's Scriptures:

"The angel said, "Don't be afraid. I'm here to announce a great and joyful event that is meant for everybody, worldwide...They left, running, and found Mary and Joseph, and the baby lying in the manger. Seeing was believing. They told everyone they met what the angels had said about this child." (Luke 2:10, 16-17, Message)

Head
Thought to Ponder:

"Seeing is believing." The shepherds came to believe when they had the opportunity to see Jesus for themselves, and their lives were never the same. As Christmas approaches, let others see your joy over the miracle of Christmas so that they might believe that there is hope for the world, a chance to experience peace, and an opportunity to experience new life for themselves, their families and their future.

So, welcome Christ into your day and look for a reason to be joyful. Then, share your joy with others through a smile, a kind greeting, a word of encouragement, and an act of kindness. No one will believe it if believers don't show it.

Heart
Invitation to Pray:

Dear Lord, we praise You for bringing hope and joy into the world. Help us share that joy with others today through our words and actions. Amen.

Song to Sing:
> Go, tell it on the mountain, over the hills and everywhere;
> Go, tell it on the mountain that Jesus Christ is born
> While shepherds kept their watching o'er silent flocks by night,
> behold throughout the heavens there shone a holy light.

Hands

Pick one or two activities that can help you and your family keep a Christ-centered focus.

Refrigerator Raid After church sometime this month, plan to find someone you don't know well and invite them over for a "Refrigerator Raid" after the service. No need to plan ahead. Just have them come straight over. Enjoy experimenting and relaxing together. Be willing to be vulnerable (don't clean your house beforehand). Just open the fridge and the cupboards and see what you can create. As you share a meal, share the joy of a new friendship.

Sharing the Legend Share the joy of a tasty Christmas treat along with the story behind it. Attach the story below to individual candy canes. Keep a handful of them with you (and your children) throughout the season so that you can pass the joy along. Surprise clerks at the shopping mall—every time you pay, give a clerk a candy cane. Take some candy canes and other Christmas goodies to your closest fire station and share the joy. Keep your eyes open for people you encounter everyday but perhaps don't really see—share the joy with them as well.

The Legend of the Candy Cane
A number of years ago, a candy maker in Indiana decided to create a candy that would tell the story of Jesus. He began with a stick of white candy to represent the purity of Christ and his sinless life. Next, he added a large red stripe to symbolize the blood Jesus shed on the cross. Then he added smaller red stripes to represent the lashes from the soldiers' whips across Jesus' back and the promise that "by His stripes we are healed (Isaiah 53:5). The candy's hardness represents that Jesus is the Rock of our salvation. The bent cane looks like the letter "J" for Jesus, and also looks like a shepherd's crook—reminding us that Jesus is the Good Shepherd.

Giving from
the Heart

Today's Scriptures:

"For God so loved the world that <u>he gave</u> his one and only Son, that who-ever believes in him shall not perish but have eternal life." (John 3:16)

"The world of the generous gets larger and larger; the world of the stingy gets smaller and smaller." (Proverbs 11:24, Message)

Head
Thought to Ponder:

As children, we loved Christmas Day because of all the gifts that were waiting for us. But as parents, we often love giving gifts more than we love receiving them. We love to see the joy on our children's faces as they open their presents, because our gifts are expressions of our love.

But the hustle and bustle of the Christmas season can suck the love right out of us. So where can we go to get recharged? We go to the Good News that "God so loved us that <u>He gave</u> his only Son." When you feel the love slipping away, repeat that verse in your mind to get refocused.

Then, offer a smile to the person who bumped into you, a kind word to someone who snapped at you, a prayer for someone who cut you off. These are gifts of love that welcome Christ to be with you in those mo-ments. A loving response may help someone else refocus on the joy of Christmas, and it might just save your evening if that snappy person hap-pens to be your spouse.

Heart
Invitation to Pray:

Father, thank You for loving us so much that You gave the costliest gift ever given—Your own Son. Today, help us to remember the depth of Your love for us, and help us to welcome You into our world by giving Your love away to others. Amen.

Hands

Pick one or two activities that can help you and your family keep a Christ-centered focus.

Be anonymous   Help someone celebrate by asking God to put on our heart the name of a person who could use a little extra money at the last minute to make ends meet this Christmas. Maybe it's a single parent or older person. Arrange to give your gift anonymously so that the recipient perceives this help as coming from the Lord.

Adopt A Child   Compassion International and World Vision are two excellent organizations that can help you "adopt" a child from another country by providing monthly support for that child's food, clothing, education and spiritual growth. Go online to learn more, then begin making a huge difference in the life of a child. Symbolically include them in all your holiday activities by putting a chair at the table with their picture on it, praying for them, writing them letters, and sending a Christmas gift.

The Real St. Nicholas   Tell your kids the story of the real St. Nicholas, who lived in the city of Myra (in modern day Turkey) in the Third Century and was a Bishop in the Church. You can go online or check your local Christian bookstore for stories about his acts of generosity that eventually led people to call him "Saint" Nicholas. He's a great model of giving from the heart.

Santa "Nose" If You've Been Good   To play the "Santa's Nose" relay game, cut small circles out of red construction paper. The first person in each line puts Vaseline on their nose, runs to the other end of the room where they stick a red "nose" onto the Vaseline, then runs back to their line without touching their nose. If they drop their nose on the way, they have to go back and start again.

A Stocking for Jesus   Here's one way to give a gift to Jesus. Hang an extra stocking for Jesus and have everyone write Him a Christmas note about how they want to be next year. After Christmas, save the notes to re-read next Christmas.

Being Present

Today's Scriptures:

"(Martha) had a sister, Mary, who sat before the Master, hanging on every word he said. But Martha was pulled away by all she had to do in the kitchen. Later, she stepped in, interrupting them. 'Master, don't you care that my sister has abandoned the kitchen to me? Tell her to lend me a hand.'

The Master said, 'Martha, dear Martha, you're fussing far too much and getting yourself worked up over nothing. One thing only is essential, and Mary has chosen it.'" (Luke 10:39-42)

Head
Thought to Ponder:

If ever there's a time you can be "pulled away" from Jesus by all the things that need to be done, it's Christmastime. But there is no more important time to "be a Mary." If we never slow down to be present with our family, friends, and especially with God, we'll never experience the miracle of Christmas—God's presence with us. Mary chose to be present, and Jesus said that was the only thing that was essential.

In the days remaining until Christmas, remember what's essential. It's not the decorating, baking, parties, or getting cards sent. There's nothing wrong with those things—they can be great ways to celebrate Christ's birthday. But what's most important is being fully present, giving the best of your energy and attention to family and friends, and spending time with God. That will be the most important present you'll give this Christmas.

Heart
Invitation to Pray:

Dear Jesus, thank You for Your invitation to simply be present with You. Thank You for the gift of Your presence with me this season. Help me today to recognize what's most important and to let the rest go. Amen.

Hands

Pick one or two activities that can help you and your family keep a Christ-centered focus.

Uni-Tasking   Many of us are expert multi-taskers. We pride our-selves in our ability to do several things at once, which can be a great asset during the Christmas season. But many of us need to develop the lost skill of being uni-taskers. Uni-tasking is the art of truly being present. It involves showing up in one place at one time, focusing on one thing. Give yourself and others the gift of uni-tasking one day this week. Truly be present. Block out distractions. Turn off your cell phone. Tune into what's going on inside you and what's going on with others around you. Welcome others into your life by offering the gift of yourself and your un-divided attention.

Christmas Freeze Dance   This is a fun game to play with your kids (or with the young at heart). Pull out some favorite Christmas music (Alvin and the Chipmunks can be a fun one), and crank up the music. While the music plays, everyone dances and jumps around. When the designated person stops the music, everyone has to freeze in whatever position they happen to be in at the moment. See who can stay frozen the longest. See who looks the funniest or silliest. Besides being great exercise and providing lots of laughs, this is a great way to simply "Be present" with your family.

Have an "Un-event"   This is an unstructured Christmas party where people just come and bring food and a story to share (perhaps a story about a favorite Christmas past). Keep it simple. Or, hold a pro-gressive dinner, with part of the meal at each person's house. This will give your group the chance to enjoy the décor at each person's home, and the chance to feel welcomed into your home—no matter how tidy or decorated it may/may not be. Simply be together.

Christmas Book Tradition   For families with young children , start a tradition of giving a Christmas book early in December. Read it to-gether and give a new book each Christmas season.

Creating Space for Others

Today's Scriptures:

"For I was hungry and you gave me something to eat, I was thirsty and you gave me something to drink, I was a stranger and you invited me in, I needed clothes and you clothed me, I was sick and you looked after me, I was in prison and you cam to visit me." (Matthew 25:35-36)

"Keep on loving each other as brothers. Do not forget to entertain strangers, for by so doing some people have entertained angels without knowing it." (Hebrews 13:1-2)

Head
Thought to Ponder:

If you are to welcome Christ, be open to surprises, or find time to simply be present, you need to create some space in your life. First, you need to create space in your heart and in your day for the Savior, and then you need to create space to welcome others. As scripture tells us, when we reach out to those in need, we are actually serving Jesus Himself. And as we read in Hebrews, when we reach out to strangers we might actually be serving an angel.

As you go through your day today, look for opportunities to welcome the Lord by creating space for others. Maybe you need to take some of the items on your "To Do" list and place them on your "To Don't" list so that you have a bit more margin in your day to connect with others. Ask God to open your eyes to the opportunities He will bring today to welcome Him by welcoming others.

Heart
Invitation to Pray:

Lord Jesus, when You arrived on earth, there was no room in the inn. Help me to not make the same mistake. Help me welcome You by opening up my heart and my time to others today. Give me eyes to see the opportunities to serve and welcome You by welcoming others. Amen.

Hands

Pick one or two activities that can help you and your family keep a Christ-centered focus.

Observe Travelers   Spend an evening at a nearby airport, train terminal, or bus station. Get a bite to eat and then go people-watching. Talk to your children about how Joseph and Mary had to take a long, tiresome trip during the time she was expecting Jesus. Pray for people you see, and look for ways to minister to weary travelers.

Birthday Party for Jesus   Throw a children's party this weekend for friends who have young children. This will give your friends several hours to decorate, bake, shop, and wrap gifts—and it will be a loving way to serve them. Help the kids make cards and gifts for their family. Play games, decorate cookies, read Christmas stories. Be sure to sing "Happy Birthday" to Jesus and eat birthday cake.

Angels in Our Midst   Angels were an important part of the Christmas story, bringing Good News about what God was doing and pointing people to God. Be an angel today by looking for someone who needs help: a friend with young kids; a single parent; an elderly person who needs someone to do some shopping for them; an ill person who needs their home cleaned. Try to find someone you can surprise with God-sent help. Set this day aside to let God use you to provide a divine encounter for someone else. You'll be surprised at how you see God working in your life as well.

Angel Prints   Remember that by serving others, we may be entertaining angels without knowing it. Help your kids be on the lookout today for "angels" they can serve and care for. Print pictures of Christmas angels or buy a set of Christmas cards or gift tags with angels on them. Hide them throughout the house and have the kids look for them throughout the day. At the end of the day, talk about the ways they saw God that day and the opportunities they had to serve someone else. Write these on the back of the angels, and use them as a visual reminder of how God showed up through others. Display your angels on the refrigerator, or strung as a Christmas garland.

~ Third Week of Advent ~

Paying Attention

to the Lord

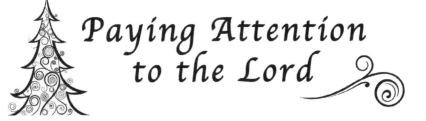

Paying Attention to the Lord

Questions to Discuss over the Sunday Meal

Gather with family or friends over a meal and talk together about how you can pay attention to the Lord as you celebrate a Christ-centered season. For families with younger children, select which questions will be most appropriate.

1. Most of the people of Bethlehem went about their business as usual that first Christmas Eve, never realizing that the Savior's birth was taking place. What are some of the business-as-usual activities you're facing this week that might keep you from paying attention to God and celebrating the wonder of Christ's birth?

2. What has happened in the last week that is keeping you from remembering that Christ's birthday is coming?

3. We pay for many things with our time and our money. But of all the kinds of payments we make, paying attention can often be the most challenging. When do you find it easiest to pay attention to God? When is it most difficult?

4. How have you heard God speak to you in the past (through a message, a song, a circumstance, a friend, an assurance in your heart, a verse of scripture, other)? How did you recognize His voice?

5. How can we pay attention a bit each day to Christ and prepare our hearts to hear from Him? What do you need to do today to ensure that you take time to pay attention to Jesus and listen for His voice?

6 If Jesus were sitting across the table from you right now, what would you want to say to Him? What do you think He might say to you?

Paying Attention to the Lord

Advent Candle Lighting
for families with young children (read the following out loud)

Parent: *(Before you begin, hide figures from the nativity set or pictures of the "Christmas characters" around the room)* I have hidden Mary, Joseph, and the baby Jesus around the room. Now, let's hunt for them, and once you find one of them, I'll help you light an Advent candle.

Parent: *(After three candles are lit) Let's* see if we can remember what the first two candles reminded us to do. *(Let kids try to answer.)* The first candle reminded us to prepare the way of the Lord. The second candle reminded us to welcome the Lord. Today, the third candle reminds us to pay attention to the Lord.

Children: Jesus Christ is Lord!

Parent: Did you know that God wants us to hunt for Him, too? The Bible says, "seek and you will find." God wants us to keep our eyes and ears open to see and hear Him all around us everyday.

Children: Jesus Christ is Lord!

Parent: When the shepherds heard that baby Jesus was born, they went hunting to find Him. When the Wise Men saw the star, they went to search for the newborn King. They were all so happy to find Him.

Children: Jesus Christ is Lord!

Parent: The Bible says that when we seek for God, we will find Him. And when we find Him, it's so wonderful it's like lighting a candle. A light goes on in our heart. We are as happy to find God as when we're playing a game of hide and seek. God loves for us to find Him. This week, let's pay attention to God and see how many places we can find Him.

All together: Jesus Christ is Lord!

Paying Attention to the Lord

Advent Candle Lighting
for individuals, couples, or families with older children

Candlelighting: Today, as we light the third candle in our Advent wreath, God is inviting us to pay full attention to Jesus. Throughout the Bible, when God's people stopped paying attention to Him, their hearts grew cold toward God, they started focusing on themselves, and it got harder for them to hear and follow God. In our scripture today, that's what happened with King Herod—his heart had grown cold and he feared losing his power to a new king. He could no longer see and hear from God because He had stopped seeking God. But God was pleased to reveal himself to a group of wise men traveling from far off lands, simply because they were willing to seek Him. *(Light third candle)*

New Testament Scripture: Read Matthew 2:1-12

Reflection: The wise men were the first Gentiles, or non-Jews, to believe in Jesus. They are quite a contrast to Herod, whose only interest in seeking the Messiah was to kill him. Herod had the title of king, but he was not the rightful heir to the throne, having usurped power by aligning himself with Rome. If the Messiah were to take his rightful place as King, then Herod stood to lose his position and his power. Sometimes there are things in our lives, too, that keep us from seeking God—because we know that if Jesus takes His rightful place as King in our lives, then we're no longer in charge. But sadly, if we stop seeking Him, then we're unable to find Him.

Old Testament Scripture: II Chronicles 7:14

Prayer: Jesus, You are the rightful King of kings. We confess that we often try to run our lives apart from You. Please forgive us and help us today to focus on You and allow You to be Lord of our lives. Amen.

Sing: Sing or listen to a favorite Christmas carol.

Sighting His Presence

Today's Scriptures:

"The people walking in darkness have seen a great light; on those living in the land of the shadow of death a light has dawned." (Isaiah 9:2)

"What has come into being in him was life, and the life was the light of all people. The light shines in the darkness, and the darkness did not overcome it." (John 1:4-5, NRSV)

Head
Thought to Ponder:

Light is more powerful than darkness—when light enters even the darkest of rooms, the darkness is overcome. Darkness cannot quench the light, but light can cast out the darkness. What a powerful metaphor for the work of God in our lives!

When Christ was born, God's great light dawned upon the world and things have never been the same. The powers of darkness that once kept people living in fear, isolation, and hopelessness were sent packing. And the same is true for us—whenever the light of Jesus shines in our lives, the darkness flees.

Where in your life do you see the light of Christ? Where do you notice Him shining in your life today, encouraging you to trust Him, giving you hope that He is truly God no matter the circumstances? Ask Him for eyes to truly see Him today. Ask Him to help you focus on the beauty of His light shining in and around you.

Heart
Invitation to Pray:

Lord Jesus, You are the light of the world. Please come shine in me and through me today. Give me eyes to recognize You today and to see the ways you are at work. And give me a heart to follow You closely. Amen.

Song to Sing:
> O, star of wonder, Star of night. Star with royal beauty bright
> Westward leading, still proceeding. Guide us to thy Perfect Light

Hands

Pick one or two activities that can help you and your family keep a Christ-centered focus.

Jesus Treasure Hunt Go through one entire day and see how many places and ways you can see Jesus (in songs, decorations, conversations, etc.). Where does He show up in surprising or unexpected ways? Over dinner, compare notes with your family and count the ways you saw Him.

Invisible Ink Write a message using lemon juice and cotton swabs. When you're ready to have it revealed, hold it up to a light bulb (or near a toaster). The heat source will slowly turn the paper dark brown and the message will be revealed. This is just like the mystery of Christ. It is always present but people cannot always see it. We help bring the mystery and beauty of Christ to light when we shine our light.

Make Luminaries Whenever you're expecting guests, light the way with luminaries. Supplies: glass canning jars, sand, tea candles, ribbon/ raffia. Put sand in the bottom of the canning jars and place tea candles on top of the sand. Wrap ribbon or raffia around the mouth of the jar. Place jars along the driveway, sidewalk or path to your front door, light the candles, and enjoy!

Flashlight Tag Turn out all the lights and give every family member a flashlight. Shine the lights on the ceiling and take turns being "it". Everyone else has to keep their light moving to avoid being tagged by "it".

Stargazing Many planetariums show journeys of the wise men at this time of year—enjoy this opportunity as a family. Or simply go stargazing together, or go to www.Hubblesite.org to see the extraordinary images taken by the Hubble telescope. Talk about the wise men who, in order to worship Jesus, followed through on what they knew was important. Some scholars say it was a two-year journey, but through it all they kept their eyes focused on the star's light. Let the night stars be a constant reminder for you and your family to follow through on what you've decided is important this season.

Hearing His Voice

Today's Scriptures:
"Suddenly a great company of the heavenly host appeared with the angel, praising God and saying,
'Glory to God in the highest,
And on earth peace to men on whom his favor rests.'" (Luke 2:13)

"When (the shepherds) had seen him, they spread the word concerning what had been told them about this child, and all who heard it were amazed at what the shepherds said to them." (Luke 2:17-18)

Head
Thought to Ponder:

The Gospel is Good News, but the sound of that Good News can get drowned out this time of year. Horns honking, commercials blaring, kids whining, and the noise in our own heads pounding. It can be tough to hear God through it all. God often speaks with a still, small voice, inviting us to pause and listen—and sometimes we have to get still ourselves before we're able to hear and understand what He's saying. But quite honestly, that's hard to do!

As you go through your day, ask God to give you a quiet heart so that no matter how much noise may be all around you, your heart will be at rest and able to hear from God. When you're in conversations with others, pay attention to Christ's presence there with you and include Him in the conversations, listening with one ear to the conversation and with your other ear to the Lord.

Heart
Invitation to Pray:

Lord Jesus, thank You for continually speaking into my life. Please help me to hear Your voice today and to discern what You're saying. Amen.

Hands

Pick one or two activities that can help you and your family keep a Christ-centered focus.

Listen Up! Help your kids learn to listen for God's "still, small voice" with this object lesson. Blindfold one child and tell them they need to follow the sound of your voice to find the candy you've hidden. Meanwhile, have everyone else yell, bang pots, etc., to try and drown out your voice. After each one has had a turn following your voice amidst the distractions, talk about how we can listen for God's voice even when there's lots of noise around us.

An Angel Gets Its Wings In the movie "It's a Wonderful Life," George Bailey learns that every time a bell rings an angel gets its wings. This week, listen for bells and ring tones and let it be a reminder to you of the Good News the angels sang about on that Holy Night when Jesus was born. Consider setting a bell tone alarm on your phone to remind you periodically throughout the day of Christ's presence with you. And just for fun, maybe watch "It's a Wonderful Life" with your family to help you remember the ways God has blessed you.

The Ho-Ho-Ho Game Have the first person lay down on their back on the floor. Have the second person lay down (perpendicular to the first person) with their head resting on the first person's tummy. Have the third person lay down (perpendicular to the second person) with their head resting on the second person's tummy, and so on, till everyone is laying on the ground with their head on someone's tummy. The object of the game is to see how long you can go before everyone breaks into giggles (it usually doesn't take long once people's heads start bouncing up and down on each other's tummies). Wipe the smiles off your faces and have the first person say Santa's famous word: "Ho." Then have the second person say, "Ho, ho." The third person says, "Ho, ho, ho," and so on. Then enjoy a good Christmas giggle.

Do You Hear What I Hear? The angels announced the birth of Christ and then they broke into song. Follow their lead and make a joyful noise by taking your family and friends Christmas caroling at a local nursing home. Be sure to sing "Angels We Have Heard on High," and "Hark the Herald Angels."

Tasting God's Goodness

Today's Scriptures:

"Taste and see that the Lord is good." *(Psalm 34:8)*

"Then Jesus declared, 'I am the bread of life. He who comes to me will never go hungry, and he who believes in me will never be thirsty.'"
(John 6:35)

Head
Thought to Ponder:

Jesus was born in the city of Bethlehem. The name "Bethlehem" means "house of bread," which is an appropriate place for Jesus, the "bread of life," to enter the world. As the bread of life, Jesus is the stuff of everyday life that we need to live on. But God does more than merely sustain us—He gives us good things to enjoy.

Today, anytime you eat or drink something, thank God for being your Provider. And thank Him for His good gift of taste buds that allow you to enjoy His provision. Pay close attention to the flavors of the foods you eat today—and let it remind you of how good God is. And also remember that Jesus, the "bread of life," is the best gift of all. And He tastes good!

Heart
Invitation to Pray:

Lord Jesus, I thank You for being my Provider and for giving me good things to enjoy. Remind me of the ways You have faithfully provided for me in the past and help me to trust You more to provide for my needs today. Please help me to taste and see just how good You are. Amen.

Hands

Pick one or two activities that can help you and your family keep a Christ-centered focus.

Pinecone Ornament Treat   Jesus said, "do not worry about your life, what you will eat or drink...is not your life more important than food? ...Look at the birds of the air; they do not sow or reap...yet your heavenly Father feeds them.   Are you not much more valuable than they?" (Matthew 6:25-26) To help you remember how much God loves you and desires to provide good things, go to a park and collect pinecones. Then make a pinecone birdfeeder by smearing peanut butter on the pinecone, covering it with birdseeds, and hanging it from a tree in your yard. Watch as the birds enjoy your tasty treat and thank God for providing you with good things

The Taste of Forgiveness   Jesus was born so that one day He could die and offer us forgiveness and new life. To help you taste the good gift of forgiveness, place a piece of unsweetened baking chocolate on your tongue and let it slowly dissolve. The bitter taste will quickly become overpowering, and you may need to spit it out. This is a reminder of what sin tastes like—its bitterness separates us from God. Then put a piece of sweetened chocolate on your tongue and let it slowly dissolve. As the taste is released, thank Jesus for coming to earth and offering the sweet gift of forgiveness.

Peppermint wreaths   Create a peppermint ornament to hang on your tree as a reminder to "taste and see that the Lord is good." Unwrap several red & white Christmas peppermint candy disks. Place them in a circle (like a wreath) on parchment paper—with the pieces just touching each other. Place in the oven at 250 degrees until peppermints start to melt together. Remove from oven and let cool completely, then tie a ribbon on the wreath and hang it up on the tree.

Edible Christmas Cards   Roll out sugar cookie dough and cut into card-sized rectangles. Decorate these "cards" with icing and Christmas messages of God's love. Deliver these tasty reminders of God's love to someone who needs some encouragement today.

Smelling the Aroma of Christ

Today's Scriptures:

"After coming into the house they saw the Child with Mary His mother; and they fell to the ground and worshiped Him. Then, opening their treasures, they presented to Him gifts of gold, frankincense, and myrrh." (Matthew 2:11, NASB)

"But thanks be to God, who always leads us in triumphal procession in Christ and through us spreads everywhere the fragrance of the knowledge of him. For we are to God the aroma of Christ among those who are being saved and those who are perishing." (II Corinthians 2:14-15)

Head
Thought to Ponder:

Gold, frankincense, and myrrh may seem like unusual gifts to give a baby, but this was no ordinary child. The wise men knew this, so they brought gifts fit for the King of kings. In addition to these costly, aromatic gifts, the wise men offered Jesus what He truly deserved—their worship. This must have been the sweetest scent to God that day.

In our reading from II Corinthians today, the Bible also tells us that when we have Christ living in us, our very lives become a fragrant aroma of God's love to the world around us. We literally "smell" like Jesus.

Today, pay attention to the Lord by noticing the aromas you encounter. Let each sweet scent remind you of the presence of the Lord. And then, like the wise men, offer up your praise and worship to Him. As you go through your day, also ask God to help you spread the life-giving aroma of Christ to others around you.

Heart

Invitation to Pray:

Lord Jesus, today help me focus on You and worship you like the wise men. And help me to spread the sweet aroma of Your presence to those I encounter. Amen.

Hands

Pick one or two activities that can help you and your family keep a Christ-centered focus.

Cinnamon Ornaments   Just as the Wise Men brought fragrant gifts to Jesus, you can fill your home with the fragrance of these easy-to-make cinnamon ornaments. Ingredients: 1 cup applesauce, 1 1/2 cup ground cinnamon, and 1/3 cup white glue. Stir ingredients together, form into a ball, and chill for 30 minutes or until dough stiffens. Sprinkle more cinnamon on cutting board or waxed-paper lined surface. Roll out dough to 1/4" thickness. Cut shapes with assorted cookie cutters. Use plastic drinking straw to make a hole through the top of each cutout. Place on cooling rack and allow to dry for about 2 days. Then put ribbon through the hole and hang your ornament.

The Aroma of Christ to Those in Transition Ask God to help you become the "aroma of Christ" to someone going through some kind of transition. Reach out to someone who has lost a loved one, lost a job, lost their home, etc. Bring them some Christmas goodies, invite them to join you for a church Christmas program, or find another way to serve them this season. Brainstorm with your family who you can reach out to and think of one way to share the love of Christ. If you are someone who has experienced loss this year, allow yourself to receive Christ's love through others today.

Name That Smell   Play a smelly game with your kids. Collect a number of "smelly" items and place them in a large sealed container. Blindfold your kids and then hold up one "smelly" item at a time under their noses. Have them take a whiff and try to guess what they're smelling. Here's some items you may want to include in your game: coffee, branch from a pine tree, dirty socks, oranges, cleaning solution, fish, sugar cookies, mustard, cinnamon, soil, baseball mitt, potpourri, etc. Give a prize to the one who guesses the most correctly.

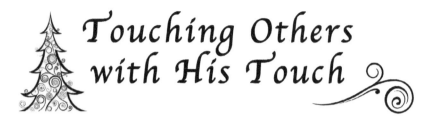

Touching Others with His Touch

Today's Scriptures:

"Then little children were brought to Jesus for him to place his hands on them and pray for them. But the disciples rebuked those who brought them.

Jesus said, 'Let the little children come to me, and do not hinder them, for the kingdom of heaven belongs to such as these.' When he had placed his hands on them, he went on from there." (Matt. 19:13-15)

Head
Thought to Ponder:

The fact that God sent His Son to earth as a flesh-and-blood person shows how much God longs to personally touch His people. Our God is an up-close-and-personal-God who wants to get close to us so that we can get close to Him.

When Jesus grew up, He continued to show His deep love for us by reaching out and touching people wherever He went. He touched lepers, a dead girl, a blind man, and tax collectors. He touched rich and poor, Jew and Gentile, young and old. When others tried to prevent Him from being the God who touches, He said, "Let the little children come to me."

Today, Jesus wants to touch your life. Stay open to the ways He may show up through the word or touch of someone else. Then ask Him to help you "be Jesus" to someone else and pass His loving touch along.

Heart
Invitation to Pray:

Lord Jesus, You weren't afraid to get Your hands dirty. You came to where people were hurting or broken and you touched them, healed them, loved them. Please touch me today and help me to pass Your touch to others. Amen.

Hands

Pick one or two activities that can help you and your family keep a Christ-centered focus.

Heart-shaped Pretzel Hugs   When you look at a pretzel in one direction, it looks like a heart—and if you turn it upside down it looks like arms wrapped around someone in a hug. Make some special chocolate heart-shaped hugs to share. Melt semi-sweet chocolate chips and dip pretzels into them; then lay pretzels on wax paper until the chocolate hardens. Think of someone who may need a "hug" today and deliver some hugs in a gift box. You may want to give some to that new neighbor who just moved in and is living far from their family this Christmas.

Mirror of God's Love   Surprise your family by leaving them a love note on the bathroom mirror before they wake up. Dry erase markers work well.

Group Hug   Gather the whole family together before bedtime for a group hug. Imagine you are the arms of Jesus, wrapping each other up in God's love. Tell each person how much you love them, and pray a prayer of thanksgiving over them.

Angel Tree   Here's a way to touch some needy kids with God's love. Go to www.angeltree.org to learn more about the Angel Tree ministry which provides Christmas gifts to children who have parents in prison. These kids need to know the love of Christ this Christmas, and you can help reach out and touch them by donating gifts.

Redefine Your Idea of "Family"   Some of us are blessed with many loving family members who live with us or near us. But others of us may not be so fortunate. Consider redefining your idea of family and finding others to touch with Christ's love this season. Find ways to include people in your Christmas celebrations who may not have family to be with. God calls us His children, so we're really all one big family anyway!

Noticing Signs of Immanuel

Today's Scriptures:

"Therefore the Lord himself will give you a sign: The virgin will be with child and will give birth to a son, and will call him Immanuel." (Isaiah 7:14)

"This will be a sign to you: You will find a baby wrapped in cloths and lying in a manger." (Luke 2:12)

"Let us fix our eyes on Jesus, the author and perfecter of our faith." (Hebrews 12:2)

Head
Thought to Ponder:

Have you ever had the experience of buying a new car, and suddenly it seems like everyone else is driving the same type of car? You begin to see them everywhere. This is called "selective attention," and it refers to the fact that we have a limited ability to pay attention to things. When you make a new purchase of any kind, your attention has now become heightened toward that item, which causes you to take more notice of it wherever you go. In reality, those cars were always there, but now you're actually noticing them.

Perhaps this week as we've been paying more attention to God, you've noticed the idea of selective attention at work. As you've tuned into His presence, perhaps you've begun to notice Him everywhere. The truth is that God is everywhere, constantly present and moving in our lives. He is Immanuel, God with us— but we need to practice noticing Him. What are the signs today of His presence with you?

Heart
Invitation to Pray:

Thank You, God, that You are always with me. You are a big God who is everywhere at once—and at the same time You are a personal God who cares about every detail of my life. Today, help me to notice Your bigness and Your awesome power, and help me to notice Your closeness and care in my life. Amen.

Hands

Pick one or two activities that can help you and your family keep a Christ-centered focus.

Signs of His Presence   Signs are meant to point us to something. There are lots of signs in our lives—billboard signs, street signs, signs of changing weather, signs of the times (economic, moral, etc) and so on. Signs are useful if we follow them. Today, what signs do you notice that point you to God? What signs are there of God's presence with you?

Noticing Him Through Others   Open your heart and home to people who may not have the option of being with loved ones this season—international students, elderly folks, military personnel. Ask God to open your eyes to those in your church or neighborhood who will be alone this Christmas. Welcome them into your celebration and when you do, look for ways God is at work in and through your time together. When extending them invitations, ask them to bring along a little Christmas of their own (i.e. a word about their own Christmas traditions, a batch of cookies, a favorite ornament, etc.) and ask them to share why it's special.

God Sightings   At dinnertime, have each family member share their "highpoint" and "lowpoint" of the day. Then talk together about where God was in those highs and lows. How was He present and working in those situations? What might God have been saying through those experiences? Then turn out all the lights and have each person light a candle for every way they saw God working today. Soon the glow of His presence will fill the room.

Divine Interruptions   Today, anytime you experience an interruption, ask God to help you see it as a divine encounter. Ask Him to help you use these as opportunities to extend His love and grace.

~ Fourth Week of Advent ~

Worshiping
the Lord

Worshiping the Lord

Questions to Discuss over the Sunday Meal

Gather with family or friends over a meal and talk together about how you can worship the Lord and celebrate a Christ-centered season. For families with younger children, select which questions will be most appropriate.

1. What are some of your favorite Christmas praise songs? What are some of your other favorite praise songs (i.e. not just for Christmas)?

2. What parts of the Advent and Christmas season help you worship God most easily? Which parts of the season make it challenging for you to worship God?

3. How do you know when you are truly worshiping—not merely going through the motions, but really adoring God with your heart, soul, mind, and strength?

4. What circumstances are you facing this year that are less than ideal? How can you make certain to worship God no matter the circumstances?

5. Have you ever felt, once Christmas was over, that in the midst of the activity you had missed celebrating Christ's birthday? How can you make sure that doesn't happen this year?

~ Fourth Sunday of Advent ~

 Worshiping the Lord

---

Advent Candle Lighting

for families with young children (read the following out loud)

Parent: *(Parent lights the first three candles or assists child to light them.)* Let's see if we can remember what the first three candles reminded us to do before we light the fourth one. *(Let kids try to answer.)* The first candle reminded us to prepare the way of the Lord. The second candle reminded us to welcome the Lord. The third candle reminded us to pay attention to the Lord. And today we will light the fourth candle to remind us to worship the Lord.

Children: Glory to God in the highest!

Parent: We can remember to worship and praise God this Christmas even if things aren't perfect. We might be tired on Christmas. Or sick. Maybe we won't get all the presents we want. Maybe we won't get to see our favorite friends or relatives. But we can still celebrate and praise God.

Children: Glory to God in the highest!

Parent: Remember the first Christmas? It had some hard parts, too. Mary and Joseph had to take a long, tiring journey, and then there was no room for them in the inn. But still they worshiped God.

Children: Glory to God in the highest!

Parent: As we light the fourth candle, let's promise to worship God no matter what, even if things aren't perfect. Let's remember that Christmas is really all about Christ—and we want to celebrate Him no matter what.

(Light the fourth candle)

All together: Glory to God in the highest!

Sing: "O Come, All Ye Faithful!"

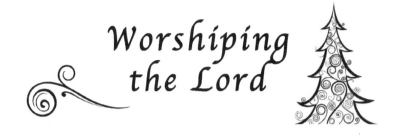

Worshiping the Lord

Advent Candle Lighting

for individuals, couples, or families with older children

Candlelighting: As we light the fourth candle, the season of Advent is drawing to a close. Let this candle symbolize the truth that we can worship the Lord no matter what circumstances we face. The first Christmas was celebrated in a stable—difficult circumstances for the birth of a child. Yet the angels sang. The shepherds worshiped. And Mary and Joseph delighted in the coming of God's newborn King. No matter how dark the night may be, the light of Christ shines brightly. *(Light fourth candle)*

New Testament Scriptures: Read Luke 2:8-20

Reflection: The word "worship" has gradually come to mean something much less than what the Bible means by it. We tend to think of a Sunday morning church service—and more specifically, we tend to think of the part of the service where we sing songs of worship. Yes, music is one way to worship God, but true worship involves our total selves—our head, heart, and hands—giving thanks, honor, and praise to our God who is worthy. The Bible calls us to worship God not only in song, but also in our thoughts, in our actions, in our celebrating, in our working, and in the ways we treat one another. We can worship God anywhere, anytime—no matter what our circumstances, no matter whether we're tired, sick, stressed, out of work, or all alone. God is still God. He is still good. And He is Immanuel, God with us. O come, let us adore Him!

Prayer: Lord God, we praise You for being our good God who loves us. You are our Provider and Protector. Today we choose to trust in You, no matter what the day or week may bring. Amen.

Old Testament Scripture: Psalm 95:3-7

Sing: Sing or listen to a favorite Christmas carol.

Surrendering Everything

(If today is December 25, skip ahead to Christmas Day on page 74)

Today's Scriptures:
"For all have sinned and fall short of the glory of God." (Romans 3:23)

"For the wages of sin is death, but the gift of God is eternal life in Christ Jesus our Lord." (Romans 6:23)

"If you confess with your mouth, 'Jesus is Lord,' and believe in your heart that God raised him from the dead, you will be saved." (Romans 10:9)

Head
Thought to Ponder:

Today's verses are all found in the book of Romans. They have been called "The Roman's Road" because they map out the road to salvation through Jesus Christ. These are great verses to commit to memory for your own encouragement, and to be able to share with others whenever God may give the opportunity to lead someone to faith.

The ultimate reason why Jesus was born 2,000 years ago was not so that we could have a big birthday celebration for Him. He came so that we could be forgiven for our sins, experience new life, and have a relationship with God. If you, or anyone in your family, have never invited Christ to be your Savior and Lord, let today be your spiritual birthday. Pray the prayer below from your heart—then tell a trusted Christian friend about your decision and celebrate it!

Heart
Invitation to Pray:

Lord Jesus, thank You for loving me so much that You came to earth and died for my sins. I confess that I have tried to be in control of my own life, but today I surrender control to You. Please forgive me and make me clean and new. I love You, Lord. Help me to follow You all the days of my life. Amen.

Hands

Pick one or two activities that can help you and your family keep a Christ-centered focus.

Shiny New Pennies After reading the verses for today, share with your kids that when Jesus enters a person's life, He makes them into new creations. Then illustrate what happens by dropping pennies into a solution of 1/2 cup of vinegar and 5 tablespoons of salt. Stir the pennies around, and almost instantly they will change color and look shiny and new. Remove pennies with a slotted spoon and dry them with paper towels. This is what God does when we ask His forgiveness and invite Him into our hearts—He cleans our hearts and makes us shiny and new. If your kids have never had the chance to pray and invite Jesus into their hearts, this may be a good time to lead them to do this. *(See prayer on opposite page.)*

Ribbon Reminder Surrendering everything to God can be costly— especially when it comes to surrendering our interactions with difficult people. Put a ribbon in your pocket to remind you of a difficult person in your life, or a difficult gathering that may be coming up. Each time you feel that ribbon in your pocket, use it as a reminder to pray for that person or event that is stressful for you. Surrender your expectations. Ask God to give you love and grace for that person or situation. Even though that person or gathering is difficult, it's still a gift. Remember that they are a person Christ died for. Pray for them, and for your attitude. Your mindset about Christmas will begin to change.

Follow the Star Just as the Wise Men surrendered their time and energy to follow the star and find Jesus, we can follow the star, too. Your kids will love making these glitter star ornaments. Materials: waxed paper, glitter, glue, marker . Tear off a piece of waxed paper and use the marker to draw a star it. Turn the paper over so the marker is on the bottom. Trace the star shape on the waxed paper with the glue. Be sure to make a fairly wide bead of glue. Sprinkle the glue with glitter till there is no more glue visible. Let it dry—this may take a few days. Then peel your star off the waxed paper and hang it up with ribbon.

Tuesday *Advent Week 4*

Up-sizing God in my Life

(If today is December 25, skip ahead to Christmas Day on page 74)

Today's Scriptures:

"For to us a child is born, to us a son is given, and the government will be on his shoulders. And he will be called Wonderful Counselor, Mighty God, Everlasting Father, Prince of Peace." (Isaiah 9:6)

"O Lord, our Lord, how majestic is your name in all the earth!" (Ps. 8:1)

Head
Thought to Ponder:

What's in a name? Quite a lot, actually! When God appeared to Moses in the burning bush, Moses asked God what he should call Him. God told Moses that His name is "I Am that I Am." God was basically saying, I Am the eternally existent One—I Am God. Jesus made it clear that He is God by also using the term "I Am" about Himself. He said, "I am the Bread of Life; I Am the Light of the World; I Am the Gate; I Am the Good Shepherd; I Am the Resurrection and the Life; I Am the Way, the Truth, and the Life; I Am the Vine."

When we focus on who God is and on all of His attributes, we take Him out of the box that we so often keep Him in and we begin to see Him for who He really is—a great big, mind-blowing God who is everywhere all the time, expressing Himself through His love and His creation. Who is God in your life today? Focus on His attributes and who you know Him to be—praise Him for these things and "up-size" Him to His real size in your life today.

Heart

Invitation to Pray:

Lord God, please forgive me for so often putting You in a box and limiting You in my life. Help me today to see You more for who You really are and to worship You as You deserve. And may others see You shining through my life. Amen.

Hands

Pick one or two activities that can help you and your family keep a Christ-centered focus.

"I Am" Go to iTunes or YouTube and listen to the song "I Am" by Mark Shultz. The words are powerful and a great reminder of the power and love of God in our lives.

The "Yes" Game See how many ways you can say "yes" to God today. When your tendency might be to get irritated by demands, interruptions, or requests, pause and ask God to show you the opportunity He might be giving you in these challenges. Can you say "yes" to God's invitation to enjoy the beauty of a snowstorm? Can you say "yes" to someone's need for help? Can you say "yes" to God asking you to slow down and wait for something? Think about the incredible lengths God went to in order to come to us—let your "yes" be a way of going to great lengths to worship Him in response.

What's in a name? Challenge yourself this week to learn the names of people you come in contact with whose names you many not always know (like the dry cleaner, the store cashier, or the bank teller). Begin greeting people on a first name basis. Think about names—how important they are. Look up the meanings of your own family names. What do they mean? How did you get those names? Then talk about Jesus' names.

Wednesday *Advent Week 4*

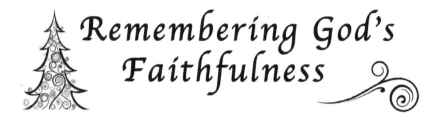

Remembering God's Faithfulness

(If today is December 25, skip ahead to Christmas Day on page 74)

Today's Scriptures:

"Of the increase of his government and peace there will be no end. He will reign on David's throne and over his kingdom, establishing and upholding it with justice and righteousness from that time on and forever. The zeal of the Lord Almighty will accomplish this." (Isaiah 9:7)

"Stand still and consider the wondrous works of God." (Job 37:14, NKJV)

Head
Thought to Ponder:

Sometimes it's easier to worship God in our present circumstances by remembering the ways we've seen God at work in the past—both in our lives and the lives of others. Take some time to think about it and ask God to bring to mind specific ways He's been at work in your life. Ask Christian friends to share stories of how they've seen God at work in the past. And spend some time in the Bible reading stories of the many ways God showed up and worked powerfully in the lives of people.

If there are places in your life where things seems confusing or you're not sure what God is up to, taking time to remember His faithfulness in the past will help you reconnect with Him. God is still God, but sometimes we forget—or have a hard time seeing it. Let Him remind you today.

Heart
Invitation to Pray:

Dear God, thank You for Your faithfulness. Help me today to remember the ways You've been at work in and around me. Help me to worship and trust You with my finances, relationships, health, future—everything I have and everything I am. You alone are God and I worship You. Amen.

Hands

Pick one or two activities that can help you and your family keep a Christ-centered focus.

Grand Memories Have your children interview their grandparents for stories of Christmases long ago. Record the interview so they can watch it again later. You might even want to post it on YouTube so the kids can share it with other family members who live at a distance. Some questions they can ask might include: How did they celebrate when they were kids? What was most fun about it? What kinds of gifts did they give? What was challenging about Christmas back then? How was it different from today? What do they miss?

Remembering Your Pastor Take time to remember those who help you worship. Pray for your pastor, church staff and their families. This can be a very busy and even overwhelming time of year for pastors—there is so much to do on top of the regular church activities. And of course, they run into many of the same challenges everyone else does with illness, family obligations, and social opportunities. Ask God to give them discernment and strength during this busy time. Pray for your pastor's family, that as they are serving others God would provide them a meaningful and joyful Christmas.

Making Family Memories Pull out old family photos, slides, and videos. Pop some popcorn and gather the family for a time of laughing and remembering. Extend the family memories by making it into a family night. Bake cookies together. Go for a walk at night and look at the stars. Make up a jump rope jingle about the birth of Jesus. Go outside and jump rope. Then come back inside and watch a Christmas movie.

Reach Out Ask God to bring to mind someone who may need an extra touch this year. Maybe they've gone through a loss this year—a loss of their home, a divorce, a death in the family, or a job loss. Simply call and say "You've been on my mind lately and I just wanted to call and see how you're doing." Let them take the lead. Just listen and be there for them.

Weighting on God

(If today is December 25, skip ahead to Christmas Day on page 74)

Today's Scriptures:

And they were calling to one another: "Holy, holy, holy is the Lord Almighty; the whole earth is full of his glory." (Isaiah 6:3)

"'I am the Alpha and the Omega,' says the Lord God, 'who is, and who was, and who is to come, the Almighty.'" (Revelation 1:8)

"'You are worthy, our Lord and God,
    To receive glory and honor and power,
For you created all things, and by your will they were created
    and have their being.'" (Revelation 4:11)

Head
Thought to Ponder:

At this time of year when we remember the birth of Jesus, it can be easy to mentally keep Him in the manger and see Him only as a baby. We can slowly begin to treat Him as being a small, fragile God—a weightless God who is cute and cuddly. But the amazing mystery and Good News of Christmas is that this little baby was fully God—and worthy of our praise.

We must remember to "weight" on God, to give Him His due and see Him as the powerful, weighty, majestic King of kings. This is what the Bible means when it says we should "magnify" the Lord. To magnify means to make larger. The truth is that God is already large, so when we magnify Him we recognize and reveal Him to be the big God He truly is.

Heart
Invitation to Pray:

God, You are worthy of our praise. Today we praise You with our lives and our hearts and our actions. May others around us see Your weightiness in our lives. Amen.

Hands

Pick one or two activities that can help you and your family keep a Christ-centered focus.

Weighty Prayers   At dinner tonight, bring out all the Christmas cards and letters you've received. Put a different Christmas card at each person's plate. During dinner, share a memory about each of the senders, then take a few minutes and pray for them. After dinner, go on a prayer walk around your neighborhood. Pray for the people you see there and thank Jesus for being the King of kings who came to earth because of His love for every one of these people.

Do You See What I See?   As we think today about seeing God for who He really is, have some fun seeing things in your home in a different way. Pull out a magnifying glass, some reading glasses or bifocals, even some drinking glasses or waxed paper, and anything else you can see through. Turn on the Christmas lights and have everyone take some type of "seeing" device. Walk through the house looking at the lights and decorations and see how different they look through these glasses.

Make a Floating Compass   Materials: Sewing needle; Magnet; Tape; wide, flat piece of cork; Plate filled with water. Magnetize the needle by stroking it with a magnet repeatedly in the same direction. Tape the needle to the center of the cork. Float the cork in the center of the water-filled plate. The needle will always point north and south. Use this to talk with your kids about how Jesus came to show us the way—in fact, Jesus said, "I Am the way, the truth and the life." When we follow Him and His directions for us in the Bible, we will always be heading in the right direction and "weighting" on God.

Friday *Advent Week 4*

Singing His Praise

(If today is December 25, skip ahead to Christmas Day on page 74)

Today's Scriptures:
"Suddenly a great company of the heavenly host appeared with the angel, praising God and saying, 'Glory to God in the highest, and on earth peace to men on whom his favor rests.'" (Luke 2:13)

"In a loud voice they sang:
'Worthy is the Lamb, who was slain,
to receive power and wealth and wisdom and strength
and honor and glory and praise!'
Then I heard every creature in heaven and on earth and under the earth and on the sea, and all that is in them, singing:
'To him who sits on the throne and to the Lamb be praise and honor and glory and power, for ever and ever!'" (Revelation 5:12-13)

Head
Thought to Ponder:

Music was part of the very first Christmas in Bethlehem as the angels joined in the chorus—and there will be an amazing concert in heaven when Christ returns. It's hard to imagine Christmas without singing. Today, raise your voice in praise to the newborn King of kings. Even if you're normally a shower only singer, take a risk today and sing to the One who is worthy to receive your praise. Or tune into your local Christian radio station and sing along with the Christmas music. (If you don't have a station in your area, go tune in online at www.KLOVE.com,)

Heart
Invitation to Pray:

O come let us adore Him, O come let us adore Him, O come let us adore Him, Christ the Lord! Amen!

Hands

Pick one or two activities that can help you and your family keep a Christ-centered focus.

Favorites on the Go   Gather everyone together and go look at Christmas lights.   While you drive, have each person pick a favorite Christmas song and sing them together. Drive slowly. Consider inviting a friend, the babysitter, a neighbor, or a senior adult to join you. Come back home for hot chocolate and treats.

Deck the Halls with Kazoos   Turn your family into a kazoo band. Pick up some cheap kazoos at a dollar store—or make your own by putting a piece of waxed paper over a comb and humming into it. Then get your family to have a "kazoo-along" of favorite Christmas carols. Surprise the neighbors by taking your band to the streets.

Hold Your Own Pageant   Encourage your kids to put on their own Christmas pageant and act out the story. This is a great way to help the story come to life in the heart of a child. Provide them with robes and sheets for costumes, a doll for baby Jesus, and a cane for the shepherds. Make crowns out of construction paper, and halos out of chenille wire. Even the family dog can get in on the act and be dressed as a lamb. Invite grandma and grandpa over and video tape the production. As someone reads the Christmas story, have the kids act it out. End by singing "Away in A Manger."

Listen to the Music   Spend a few minutes getting quiet. Turn off all the house lights and light some candles. Imagine being one of the shepherds that night on a quiet hillside, when suddenly a bright light breaks through the darkness, an angel makes a startling announcement, and then a heavenly concert breaks out.   Turn on some Christmas music and enjoy the candlelight. Read a Christmas story. Talk about favorite Christmas memories. Enjoy God's presence in your family.

Enjoying Him with Others

(If today is December 25, skip ahead to Christmas Day on page 74)

Today's Scriptures:
"When they saw the star, they were overjoyed. On coming to the house, they saw the child with his mother Mary, and they bowed down and worshiped him. Then they opened their treasures and presented him with gifts of gold and incense and of myrrh." (Matthew 2:10-11)

Head
Thought to Ponder:

As our culture becomes more secularized and commercial, some Christians are frustrated that Christ is no longer at the center of Christmas. They are upset that shop clerks no longer say "Merry Christmas" but instead say, "Season's Greetings" or "Happy Holidays." They may even get angry that their town no longer allows a nativity scene on public property. After all, Jesus is the reason for the season, right?

Yes it's true that Christ is what Christmas is really all about—but it's not true that the world is responsible to keep Christ at the center of Christmas. God's people are the ones charged to "Go Tell it on the Mountain, that Jesus Christ is born." We're the ones who spread the light of Christ by letting His light shine brightly in our own hearts. Ask yourself this question: If your neighbors watched you over this Christmas season, where would they see Jesus in your life?

Heart
Invitation to Pray:

Lord Jesus, today let us follow in the footsteps of the wise men who sacrificed time and energy to seek You out and to worship You. Please fill our hearts today with more of Your love, and may it overflow to those around us who need to know the real reason for this season. Amen.

Hands

Pick one or two activities that can help you and your family keep a Christ-centered focus.

A Tale of Heaven & Hell   There's an old tale about the difference between heaven and hell. The image of hell is that of a banquet hall, with fine china on the table, delicious food, and everyone dressed in their finest clothes. There's just one thing out of place—the utensils are overly large, too large for anyone to be able to feed themselves. In the process of people attempting to eat, they bump into each other and arguments break out. In the end, no one is able to eat anything and they're all left wanting and unsatisfied. The image of heaven begins the same way, but there's one big difference—the people. They recognize right away that they will not be able to feed themselves with the overly large utensils, so they begin to feed one another. Because the people have learned to feed one another, they are all filled and satisfied. While this story is not found in the Bible, the idea of God's people sharing and showing love toward one another is definitely God's design. Consider having fun with this story and attempting to feed one another at dinner tonight—it could make for some giggles and a great lesson on sharing.

Free Gifts   Give gifts to each other that cost nothing. Brainstorm ideas together and then have fun giving. Here's a few ideas to get you started:

1) *Listen*—really listen. Don't interrupt, day dream, or plan your response. Just listen.

2) *Laugh*—clip cartoons, share funny stories.

3) Give a compliment—look for the best in everyone. Tell them when they are doing their best. Tell them you appreciate them and why. Write it in a note.

4) *Be kind*—Go out of your way to be kind, to do something nice.

5) *Be cheerful*—Smile with your whole face. Send happy face emoticons to someone in an email to brighten their day.

Celebrating Christ
No Matter Your Circumstances

Christ Candle Lighting
Can also be lit on Christmas Eve

for Families, Couples, and Individuals

Candlelighting: The fifth and final candle of the Advent wreath is a birthday candle—sometimes called the Christ candle. Jesus is born! The lighting of the Christ candle marks the conclusion of our time of waiting and preparation. It signifies the birth of Christ in Bethlehem: the heart of the Christmas celebration. May we always rejoice at the light of this candle, because it reminds us of God's gift of salvation.
Happy birthday, Jesus!

(Light all five candles)

New Testament Scriptures: Read John 3:16; Luke 2:25-32

Reflection: Have you ever struggled to keep a gift someone has given you? Maybe you don't like it and would just prefer to exchange it. While receiving certain gifts with genuine gratitude can be difficult, Simeon shows us how to receive God's gift of salvation. His heart was overflowing with praise! Many people find it hard to receive Jesus, this great and remarkable Savior. Yet He longs to come into our lives and shower us with His love and forgiveness. Have you made room in your heart for Him this Christmas? He is the one gift that perfectly fits every human heart.

Prayer: Lord Jesus, welcome to our world! Thank You for loving us and walking with us through this Christmas season. Help us celebrate this day with You at the center of it all—and may we keep You in our hearts throughout the year. Amen.

Sing: Joy to the world!

Celebrating Christ
No Matter Your Circumstances

Flaming Birthday Cake for Jesus Celebrate Jesus' birthday with this memorable flaming treat. *Materials:* One sheet cake; Green cake frosting; Sugar cubes; Peppermint extract.

Directions:

1. Decorate a 13X9-inch sheet cake with green frosting to look like a Christmas tree (feel free to add piping, sprinkles, etc.).

2. Arrange the sugar cubes on the surface to look like lights on a tree..

3. Infuse each sugar cube with a few drops of peppermint extract just prior to igniting.

4. Turn off lights and use a match to carefully ignite the extract on each "star," moving quickly from cube to cube. Each star will burn with a pretty blue flame for about a minute.

5. Sing "Happy Birthday" to Jesus and enjoy the flaming treat.

Celebrate No Matter the Circumstances If circumstances like weather, illness, distance, or work have you alone this Christmas, don't forgo your celebration. Remember that it's Christ's birthday and you're never really alone. Make a favorite dessert even if you can't possibly eat it all yourself. Set the table with your good china, play Christmas music, enjoy a favorite book or Christmas movie, treat yourself to a long-distance call to a good friend or relative.

The Unfortunately-Fortunately Game As we all know, Christmas doesn't always turn out the way we expect. Help your kids learn to take disappointments and turn them into positives by playing the Unfortunately-Fortunately Game. Like: "Unfortunately Grandma just gave me a gift I already have. Fortunately I can be grateful because now I have something to give to a kid who doesn't have many toys." See how many unfortunates you can turn into fortunates—then praise God for His good gifts!

About The Author

Linda Sommerville is a writer, speaker, educator, spiritual director, and pastor-at-large.

She and her husband, Phil, create small group resources, inspirational books, and church campaigns through their web-based ministry, FaithAlive365. They also provide ministry coaching and spiritual growth events designed to help people come more fully alive in Christ 365-days-a-year, not just on Sundays.

Linda is a diehard Christmas fanatic (just ask Phil!), but her favorite part of the season is spending time with her husband and two sons in their home in Rocklin, CA, making memories and keeping Christ at the center of the celebrations. She would love to hear about your Christmas ideas and traditions, as well as the ways you used this Advent Guide. Please email her and share your stories.

Contact Linda: Linda@FaithAlive365.com

faithALIVE365
Living God's Best Every Day

At Faith Alive365 we are creating resources for churches, groups and individuals that will help them live God's best every day. You can find our great resources on our website or on Kindle and Nook.

www.faithalive365.com